HELPING THE TRAINABLE MENTALLY RETARDED CHILD DEVELOP SPEECH AND LANGUAGE

With a Foreword by

Edward A. Aleo, Ph.D.

Director
Elmira College Speech and Hearing Clinic
and Department of Speech and Hearing
Elmira, New York

HELPING THE TRAINABLE MENTALLY RETARDED CHILD DEVELOP SPEECH AND LANGUAGE

A Guidebook for Parents, Teachers and Paraprofessionals

By

MICHAEL LEWIS GORDON
Executive Director

DAVID H. RYAN
*Supervisor of Instruction
and Recreation*

TAMAR SHILO
*Speech and Language
Specialist*

*Chemung County Chapter
New York State Association
For Retarded Children, Inc.
Horseheads, New York*

CHARLES C THOMAS • PUBLISHER
Springfield • Illinois • U.S.A.

Published and Distributed Throughout the World by
CHARLES C THOMAS • PUBLISHER
BANNERSTONE HOUSE
301–327 East Lawrence Avenue, Springfield, Illinois, U.S.A.
NATCHEZ PLANTATION HOUSE
735 North Atlantic Boulevard, Fort Lauderdale, Florida, U.S.A.

© *1972, by* CHARLES C THOMAS • PUBLISHER
ISBN 0-398-02453-7 ✓
Library of Congress Catalog Card Number: 75-187657

With THOMAS BOOKS *careful attention is given to all details of manufacturing and design. It is the Publisher's desire to present books that are satisfactory as to their physical qualities and artistic possibilities and appropriate for their particular use.* THOMAS BOOKS *will be true to those laws of quality that assure a good name and good will.*

Printed in the United States of America
CC-11

FOREWORD

WITHIN THE LAST ten to twenty years, interest in special education has steadily increased in the professional and academic world. This increased interest has led to research investigating improvements in the educational process for physically, emotionally, neurologically, and culturally disadvantaged children. As a result of such research, refined diagnostic and rehabilitative procedures for these children have been developed.

After reviewing the literature extensively, Mr. Gordon and his associates have attempted to expand the procedural and therapeutic methods which most efficiently aid in the instruction of trainable mentally retarded children. The compiling of the data within this guide was accomplished with most sincere thoughts of including the parents in their children's education.

The exercises found in this guide follow a general sequence which helps to develop a child physiologically.

The authors have attempted to follow the sequence of natural maturation in developing activities to improve motor coordination. In essence, they suggest that in developing a child's intelligence, we must first develop awareness of his physical capabilities and his environment.

The format of this guide makes the parents a vital part of the rehabilitative program and broadens their understanding of their roles in such programs. By attempting to achieve these goals, the authors hope to bring us one step closer in bridging the gap between the education of these children in formal settings and the carryover of the procedures into the home. If Mr. Gordon's endeavors have satisfied these goals, the obvious results will be improvements in the rehabilitation and education of exceptional children.

I am sure that educators, students, and parents will find the information within these pages enlightening and helpful.

EDWARD A. ALEO, PH.D.

PREFACE

FOR MORE THAN a decade, the Chemung County Chapter, New York State Association for Retarded Children, Inc., has endeavored to improve the training available for the trainable mentally retarded child so that he may achieve full potential. Nowhere has this need for improved training existed more than in the area of speech and language training.

Parents of trainable children can tell you of their past experiences with experts in the speech and language field when they were told to "wait and he will talk" or "we can't do anything, your child doesn't have much hope." It is small wonder that parents of trainable mentally retarded children show such astonishment when their children start using speech and language.

The parents and the family of the trainable mentally retarded child play a large role in developing the child's ability to use speech and language.

One of the main reasons this guide was developed was to give parents a concrete, concise, and practical aid in guiding their children to a goal which more often than not can be attained: the development of good, useable speech and language for their trainable mentally retarded child.

As the child grows, the parents will begin to share the responsibility for training the child with people outside the home. Whether the parents choose a private day school or a residential school, or if their child is accepted in public school, the need for speech and language training continues. *Helping the Trainable Mentally Retarded Child Develop Speech and Language* bridges the gap between home and school by providing activities and exercises which will aid in the continuous development of speech and language in the trainable mentally retarded child. The guide is developed so as to provide functional resources for the teacher of the trainable child while limiting theoretical considerations to only the needed minimum for the optimal development of paraprofessionals and volunteers who are now more than ever working with trainable mentally retarded children.

We feel that *Helping the Trainable Mentally Retarded Child Develop Speech and Language: A Guidebook for Parents, Teachers, and Paraprofessionals* will help to demonstrate that the training of speech and language in the trainable mentally retarded child is the responsibility of everyone having contact with the child and, what's more, that this training does not require any more expertise than the adequate use of speech and language and the ability to read.

MICHAEL LEWIS GORDON
DAVID H. RYAN
TAMAR SHILO

INTRODUCTION

IT IS of primary importance in the educational and training process of the trainable mentally retarded child not to take anything for granted and to constantly motivate and stimulate the child's behavior. The environment of the trainable mentally retarded child might be meaningless to him unless the people in his environment change it into a learning environment.

The learning experience of the trainable mentally retarded child must therefore involve all his senses: visual, motor, auditory, sensory, and tactile.

Adequate looking and listening behavior, if not established naturally, should be a major goal in the development of language. At a later stage, looking behavior should be developed to a more skilled behavior —visual—by stimulation, experience, and reinforcement. Listening behavior should be developed simultaneously into auditory skills.

The language process can be divided into three distinct phases (Myklebust, 1969) : (1) *receptive language* which is used to understand what others say, (2) *inner language* which is used for thinking or "talking to ourselves," and (3) *expressive language* which is used in talking to others or in expressing thoughts, feelings, or ideas.

A fundamental basis of language behavior is *inner language*. It is necessary for the infant to receive verbal stimulation for a certain period of time in order to understand spoken symbols (language). After hearing and understanding these symbols for another period of time, the child then begins to use them expressively.

The sequence of language development, then, is (1) reception of language stimulation, (2) developing of inner language, and (3) development of speech or expressive language.

In order for a child to verbally communicate thoughts to others, there must be a speaker and a listener. Someone must listen, maintain interest, and give the child a feeling that he has something important to say.

It is especially appropriate in working with the trainable mentally retarded child to regard verbal behavior as part of the child's overall behavior. Verbal behavior in the trainable mentally retarded child cannot be developed unless other aspects of behavior show readiness for speech (Skinner, 1957; Buddenhagen, 1971).

CONTENTS

HELPING THE TRAINABLE MENTALLY RETARDED CHILD DEVELOP SPEECH AND LANGUAGE

Chapter I

SIGNS OF SPEECH AND LANGUAGE READINESS AND SOME DEVELOPMENTAL EXERCISES

PHYSICAL BEHAVIOR

IN ORDER for the trainable mentally retarded child to begin to use language, his body must want to and be able to express his thoughts and feelings, and his speech organs must be developed to that end.

The child must be physically capable of expanding his chest and filling his lungs with air. As his lungs collapse, the air rushes past his vocal cords producing sound. The child then converts this sound into meaningful speech and language. Proper breathing is most important for the development of speech and language. Since the trainable mentally retarded child, especially the mongoloid, is so susceptible to respiratory problems which result in a congested chest, he has potentially weak lungs and difficulties in breathing. Therefore it is very important to build and develop the trainable mentally retarded child's breathing through exercises designed to give the child practice at inhaling and exhaling.

Other physical activities such as sucking, swallowing, control of drooling, tongue control, and chewing may have to be improved before many trainable mentally retarded children can produce intelligible and meaningful speech and language.

Inhaling Exercises

- Have the child inhale at any desirable rate any amount of air up to his maximum capacity. The use of a mirror for this activity may assist the child in observing his chest expansion, shape of lips, and depressed cheeks.
- The child should be encouraged to be as noisy or as quiet as he wants while inhaling.
- Have the child inhale, hold his breath, and then release the air.
- Have the child inhale, hold his breath, puff his cheeks, and then exhale with his cheeks puffed.
- Have the child inhale as much air as he can while you count up to three, four, five.
- Hold a piece of paper touching the child's lips. Have the child inhale. The paper should stay on the child's lips as long as he inhales.

Exhaling Exercises

- Have the child blow candles, papers, cotton balls, and feathers.
- Have the child stand or sit in front of a mirror. If he gets close enough to the mirror and blows, he will be able to see his breath marks on the mirror.
- Have the child blow on a cold window during the winter so that he can see the frost marks left by his breath.

- Have the child whistle: long and short, slow and fast.

- Have the child blow on his own hand so that he may feel the force of his breath.

- Have the child blow dandelion seeds.

- Have the child exhale while you count to two, three, four.

- While the child exhales, have him feel and watch his abdominal (stomach) muscles.

- Have a blowing contest with a few children. The child who can blow the object the farthest wins. Use bubbles, balloons, party horns, whistles.

- When the child exhales, try to get him to produce a vowel sound: ah, oo, ee.

Sucking and Swallowing Exercises

- For proper sucking and swallowing, it is important to keep the head in an upright position.

- To stimulate the child to suck, compress his cheeks.

- Stroking the child's throat muscles while you are compressing his cheeks will stimulate him to swallow.

- Spooning of cold fluids will stimulate swallowing. Use nondairy unsweetened fluids such as unsweetened Kool-Aid and water.

- If the child can feed himself with a spoon, jams and jellies will help swallowing. As the child learns to swallow, introduce thicker foods.

- Lollypops can be used for rewarding and reinforcing sucking and swallowing.

- Have the child sip fluids through a straw. When he can do this with no trouble, pinch the straw.

- Ice cream can be used as a reward but it might inhibit swallowing as it is a saliva-thickening food.

Note: Warm sweet fluids, citric acids, and milk products are hard to swallow. Salty and oily fluids are easier to swallow.

Drooling Control Exercises

- Humming, kissing, humming on a piece of paper which gives a tickle-like sensation, and lip printing on a piece of paper (put lipstick on the child's lips) are good exercises which encourage the child to close his lips. Lip printing shows the child the differences between open and closed lips.

- When the child drools with his mouth open, a tap under his chin will prompt him to close his mouth.

- Have the child chew like a cow in front of a mirror.

- Have the child exercise, protruding and retracting his lower jaw, to strengthen the muscles around his mouth and improve their coordination. These exercises should be done at a slower rate with a mongoloid because of the larger size of the child's tongue.

- Biting exercises for jaw closure are important.

Tongue Control

- Apply pressure to the child's tongue with a tongue blade or a popsicle stick. Start at the tip of the tongue and work toward the back with a *walking* motion. The child's tongue will move back into his mouth automatically.

- Play *Do What I Do* with the child. Have the child imitate your tongue movements. Some good tongue exercises are trying to touch the nose, trying to touch the chin, moving the tongue laterally, and extending the tongue as far as possible and retracting the tongue. As the child improves, he may be directed to increase the speed of these individual tongue exercises.

- Have the child produce a la la la sound with an alternating slow and fast rhythm.

Chewing Exercises

- Have the child bite down so that he will leave an impression of his teeth on such substances as soft candy and gum.

- Have the child chew taffy as vigorously as possible.

- Have the child chew on a wet cloth rag so that he will suck all the water out.

LOOKING BEHAVIOR

It is very important that the child be exposed to a variety of looking experiences if he is ever to develop and use language. The training of looking behavior should begin when the child is in infancy and should be carried on indefinitely. If the child attends with the eyes, he usually is also attending with the ears.

Call Attention to Yourself

When the child looks in your direction, reward him. Use any attention-getting technique: call the child's name, clap your hands, or turn lights on and off. Use attention-getting techniques from different parts of the room. Do not hide; remain visible. The child should be able to follow you with his eyes. If the child does not respond, get closer to him. Repeat your attention-getting techniques until the child looks. Make these exercises fun games!

Call Attention to Your Face

Hold the child in your lap. Babble, tickle, laugh with him. Pause, giving the child a chance to respond. Repeat your activity after the child looks at you.

Ball Games

Roll the ball. You and the child crawl or run after it. Say, *Where is the ball* or *Look for the ball.* Then, *Here is the ball,* when you find it or catch it.

Mirror for Self-Discovery

Have a large, low-placed mirror in the room. Stand or sit in front of the mirror yourself and play with your hands and face. Make sure the child is aware of what you are doing. Name parts of the body when you touch them. If the child does not approach the mirror by himself, bring him to it.

Name *hands.* Put hands on mirror, wiggle your

fingers, and get the child to look at his hands. When the child shows some understanding of the word *hands* (by moving his hands when you say the word), proceed in the same manner to other parts of the body: nose, eyes, mouth, ears, feet. Allow the child free time at the mirror.

When the child becomes familiar with the mirror, play the game *Where is Johnny's nose? Here is Johnny's nose!* Point with your finger.

Call Attention to Food

Do not feed the child unless he looks at the food. *Be consistent.* Serve the food from different directions, thus attracting the child's attention.

Call Attention to Noisemaking Objects

If the child does not respond, encourage him by saying, *Look here.* Repeat your activities with different noisemakers only after the child has responded appropriately to one. Do not expect immediate results. Use the child's favorite noisemaker, and use one noisemaker at a time.

Ring the bell (xylophone, squeaker, etc.). Pause. Give the child a chance to look. If he looks or attempts to look ring it again as a reward.

Looking and Reaching for Objects

Hold one toy within the child's reach. Get the child's attention by calling his name. If necessary, guide his hand and face toward the toys.

Naming Pictures

Teach the child to point to the picture. Point to the

picture yourself, saying its name *(dog)*, and ask the child to *point to the dog*.

Use this technique with other dog pictures. You may use pictures which include other objects in addition to dogs. Ask the child to identify the dog.

Have a toy dog to be matched with the picture of the dog. Refer back and forth, saying, *Dog—dog*. A cloth or a felt dog for the child to feel can be most helpful. Make the dog sound, *Bow—wow*, but do not expect the child to repeat the sound.

LISTENING BEHAVIOR

Listening and looking tend to occur simultaneously. If the child is attending to sound, he is also looking. In learning the sounds in his environment and the verbal speech sounds which make up language, a child must be trained to listen.

Since looking and listening are so closely related in learning language, most of the activities used to train looking behavior can also be used to train listening behavior. Below are some additional listening exercises.

Mirror for Self-Discovery

- At the mirror have the child do the following: *Babbling*—use visual sounds, /p/, /b/, /m/, /l/, /w/; *tapping*—tap finger on mouth, producing sounds like *oo, ah, ee, oh*. Use the mirror as in looking, but stress listening.

Identifying Body Parts from Pictures

- Name the body parts for the child, then ask the child to point to the body parts that you have named. Do not give visual clues. Rely on listening skills only.

Call Attention to Yourself

- Do as in looking activities, but stress the child's listening ability. When the child responds, reward him.

Hide and Seek

- Hide a clock in the room. Ask the child to find the clock by locating the tick-tock sound. Reward the child when he finds the clock. Use other noisemaking devices to play this game.

Listening and Responding to Name

- Hold one toy within the child's reach. Get the child's attention by calling *his* name. If the child looks at you when you call his name, reward him by giving him the toy.

Call Attention to Noisemaking Objects

- Use the same techniques as in looking activities. Have the child identify the correct noisemaker from a group after he hears the sound.

IMITATING

The trainable mentally retarded child loves to imitate and enjoys others imitating his own actions. It is mainly for this reason that imitation can be a valuable teaching technique.

Since imitation of vocal behavior follows imitation of motor behavior, the child should be asked to imitate movements before he is asked to imitate vocal responses. Imitation, if used properly with the trainable mentally retarded child, will help the child to remember and will also motivate his interest. Imitation can also be a form of self-expression for the child.

Child's Imitation of Adult Behavior

Gradually introduce simple games (peek-a-boo), rhymes (patta-cake), and mirror work (see specific mirror activities under *Looking and Listening Activities*).

Do not demand or command any imitative behavior on the child's part. Play your game pleasantly and enjoy it, and hopefully the child will associate your activities with pleasant memories.

Your activities should be useful to the child and at the level of his ability. Some activities suggested for imitative games are washing hands and face, drying hands and face, combing hair, cleaning the house, hanging clothes, and wiping the nose.

Imitation of Child's Behavior

When the child crawls, crawl with him. When he claps his hands or pounds on the table, do the same. The child needs the reinforcement and the encouragement of his own behavior by himself and others.

When the child throws the ball, runs after it, or chases you, cooperate and imitate his way of playing.

Imitate the sounds made by the child. By doing this you stimulate, reinforce, and motivate the child in his activities. Make it a fun game. Apply affection and pleasure to your voice to leave the child with a pleasant association.

Gradually vary the sounds the child practices. Introduce sounds that can be used later to represent the people who are doing the training (such as *mama*).

If the child has been babbling and stops suddenly, use this silent moment to attract his attention and repeat the child's former vocalization. This is done to retain his interest.

Training should continue until the child responds consistently and repetitively to the trainer's vocal play and imitation.

EMOTIONAL AND SOCIAL BEHAVIOR

A child may be physically ready to begin using speech and language but may still remain a *nontalker*. This may be due to the child's not being *language ready* in one or more areas. In addition to having developed looking, listening, and imitative readiness, the child must be emotionally and socially ready to use language.

Before the child begins to use language, he must *want* to communicate. He must have a good feeling about himself, one that tells him that he has something to say that people will listen to. He must feel that there are people that want to talk to him. Also important is a feeling that his use of language will be accepted and not rejected. In summary, the child should have developed, or be on the way to developing, a positive self-image.

The child also should be developing some degree of social awareness. Being aware of other children and how to function socially with them will tend to motivate, stimulate, and reinforce the child's language behavior.

It is therefore most important to aid the child in developing (1) a healthy self-image, (2) good relationships with other people, (3) a stable relationship with his physical environment, and (4) a constantly developing concept and practice of socially acceptable behavior.

Chapter II

STARTING A LANGUAGE PROGRAM FOR THE TRAINABLE MENTALLY RETARDED CHILD

INGREDIENTS

Before STARTING in a language development program, the child should be diagnosed properly by professional people including the pediatrician, the otolaryngologist (ear nose throat), the audiologist, the speech pathologist, the social worker, the psychologist, and the orthodontist.

When you plan or develop language development activities, be sure to include the following seven points in your approach:

1. *Sequential Learning:* Activities, goals, and learnings are approached according to the level of difficulty, starting from the least difficult and proceeding to the more difficult, making sure that increases are gradual, successful, and well-rewarded.

2. *Learning in Small Steps:* Break each bit of learning into a small enough piece that the child will be able to digest easily and with success. Make sure that the child meets with more success than failure and is rewarded frequently and consistently.

14

3. *Adequate Interaction between the Child and the Learning Environment:* The child must be aware of his environment and that his interaction with the environment is his best learning tool. Experiences and activities should be used to develop the child's ability to move independently through his environment.

4. *Constant and Consistent Reinforcement:* Reinforcement, review, and reward of desirable behavior should be foremost in any program to develop the trainable mentally retarded child's language ability.

5. *Self-Pacing:* The progress of developmental activities should be geared to the child's level of readiness rather than the teacher's time schedule.

6. *Individual Instruction:* Activities should be developed for the individual child and on a one-to-one basis as much as possible.

7. *Constant Evaluation and Adjustment of the Goals and Content of the Program:* Individual and group results, as well as the effectiveness of the training techniques and personnel, should be constantly reviewed and improved upon.

Speech Correction for the Trainable Mentally Retarded Child

The goal of any language development program for the trainable mentally retarded child is *good, usable speech!* Since probably all trainable mentally retarded children will have some trouble making sounds properly, it is important to train the child to communicate before trying to correct a speech defect. Do not try to correct a child's lisp if he cannot yet tell you his name or when he has to go to the potty. Speech correction goals are only secondary to language development goals.

GENERAL SUGGESTIONS FOR TRAINING

Be a good model of speech for the child in the following ways:

a. Talk slowly but naturally.
b. Use proper volume and proper inflection.
c. Talk to the child, and look at him while you are talking.
d. Eliminate baby talk.
e. Be consistent and patient.

Always associate speech with fun. Remember, unpleasant communication creates an unpleasant experience which might discourage the child from trying to speak.

Too much stimulation and at the wrong time may cause the child to lose interest.

Create the need for verbal communication. Silent gestures must remain unrewarded.

Build a useful vocabulary and *use* words instead of saying them.

Review frequently, and reward desirable responses more frequently.

LANGUAGE DEVELOPMENT GOALS FOR THE TRAINABLE MENTALLY RETARDED CHILD

The most important language development goals are the following:

1. The child should be able to comprehend words for protection such as *no, don't touch, come here,* and *hot.*

2. The child should be able to state his full name and names of family members, teacher, and classmates.

3. The child should be able to use polite expressions

such as *thank you, please, sorry, excuse me, you're welcome, hi,* and *good-bye.*

4. The child should be able to listen to and respond appropriately to a short message or simple command.

5. The child should be able to express himself simply.

6. The child should be able to answer the phone.

7. The child should be able to deliver a short message.

8. The child should be able to listen and retell a short story, ask appropriate questions, and maybe make up a short story by himself.

LESSON PLAN FORMAT
For Individual or Group Lesson
Some Examples

Name of Activity: Sucking and Swallowing

Objectives

To stimulate reflex closure.
To develop muscle coordination.
To develop fine muscles.
To strengthen muscles.
To establish jaw stability.

Problem

J.J., mongoloid, trainable mentally retarded. C.A. 10, M.A. 2.6. Continuous drooler, hypotonic swallower.

Motivation

Introduction and establishment of rapport with child.
Informality.
Mirror.

Procedures

Head stability.
Lip closure.
Reflex closure.
Chewing like a cow.

Materials Needed

Mirror.

Variations

Humming.
Kissing.

Expected Outcome

With the application of these activities, the child should have better sucking and swallowing control.

Name of Activity: Self-Discovery

Objectives

To develop an awareness of the child's own body parts.
To be familiar with names of the various body parts.
To show knowledge of the function of some body parts.

Problem

E.P., trainable mentally retarded with cerebral palsy involvement. C.A. 9.3, M.A. 2.1. Shows very limited awareness of his own body parts.

Motivation

The association of pleasant stimuli with a specific body part.
Mirror.

Procedures

Teacher names and touches parts of the body.
Name and touch parts of the body in front of the mirror.
Teacher names and child touches his own or the teacher's body parts.

Materials Needed

Mirror.
Picture cards.
Flowers to smell.
Material to feel.
Noisemakers.
Candy to taste.

Variations

Picture cards or simple stick drawings on the blackboard.

Expected Outcome

With the application of these activities, the child should become more familiar with his body parts.

Name of Activity: Tongue Control

Objectives

To keep the child's tongue inside his mouth.
To stimulate reflex closure.
To strengthen facial and tongue muscles.
To establish jaw stability.

Problem

C.C., mongoloid, trainable mentally retarded. C.A.

8.6, M.A. 3.3. Slightly opened mouth and protruding tongue.

Motivation

Operant conditioning; reward for positive responses. Mirror.

Procedures

Head stability.
Lip closure.
Reflex closure.
Apply tongue blade pressure to get child to pull tongue into mouth.

Materials Needed

Mirror.
Tongue blade.

Variation

Do what I do imitation games.

Expected Outcome

With the application of these activities, the child should be able to keep his tongue within his mouth.

Name of Activity: Auditory Reception

Objectives

To develop the child's understanding of the spoken word.

Problem

F.K., trainable mentally retarded. C.A. 7.0, M.A. 3.4. Shows limited understanding of what is said to her. Echoes frequently.

Motivation

Introduction and establishment of rapport.
Informality.
Reward: candy, toys.

Procedures

The use of a limited, simple vocabulary.
Frequent repetitions for reinforcement.
Following simple directions such as touching various body parts and commands (sit down, etc.).

Materials Needed

Rewards: candy, toys.

Variations

Use a picture card of a child for the reinforcing of vocabulary taught (body parts), or a picture card of an animal.

Expected Outcome

With the application of the above activities, the child should develop an understanding of what is said to her.

Name of Activity: Visual Memory

Objectives

To develop the child's ability to remember objects

that he has seen before, and to recall their looks from his memory.

Problem

P.D., trainable mentally retarded. C.A. 6.3, M.A. 3.4. Noticeable deficit in visual memory. Has quite a bit of intelligible speech.

Motivation

Reward.
Use only familiar objects.

Procedures

Ask, *Can you make a necklace like mine?* When child succeeds, increase the difficulty by presenting a more complicated pattern.
Present three objects, then hide one. Ask the child to identify the hidden object from memory.

Materials Needed

A few objects (the more objects you use, the more difficult the exercise becomes) .
Beads.

Variations

Recall games (i.e. who is missing today) .
Production of different patterns from memory.

Expected Outcome

With the application of the above activities, the child should begin to develop or improve her visual memory.

Chapter III

DEVELOPMENTAL ACTIVITIES

THE ILLINOIS TEST of Psycholinguistic Abilities
(McCarthy and Kirk, 1963) has made a major contribu-
tion to the study, understanding, and training of language. This test and the language model on which it is
based formally recognize the distinction between receptive and expressive language. The activities which follow
are based on the psycholinguistic language model which
the I.T.P.A. tests.

Further explanation of the various language func-
tions contained in the psycholinguistic model precede
each group of activities.

AUDITORY RECEPTION

Auditory reception is the child's ability to understand
what is said to him. It is one of the most important
stages in the child's language development process. Unless the child understands the spoken word, he is unable
to do the very basic tasks, such as protecting himself
(stop, hot!) ; he is certainly unable to perform the more
complicated tasks, such as following directions, answer-
ing questions, or listening to stories.

The trainable mentally retarded child often has difficulty understanding what is said to him. The parent
and teacher can help the child develop such an under-

standing by working on the auditory reception training activities suggested below.

Repetition and reinforcement of these activities is most important for the trainable mentally retarded child, whose problem is not only the learning of the auditory reception skills, but also remembering them.

Body Parts

- Have the child touch his ear, his eye, his nose, his mouth, his hair, his foot.
- Use rhythm or songs with the touching.

Follow Simple Directions

- Give the child simple directions such as *sit down, get up, come here, don't touch, stop, look here, show me, give me, stay there, say bye-bye, open the door, close the door, lie down.*

Follow More Complicated Directions

- When the child can follow simple directions, give him directions that are more complex or that will require him to do more than one thing.
- Ask the child to touch your nose.
- Ask the child to put a block on a box, in a box, under a box, between a box and a car. Be sure that the child understands the concepts before proceeding with these directions.
- Tell the child to listen and do only what he is told: *raise your hands, stamp your feet.* Use pauses to get the child's attention.

Paper Folding

- Instruct the child to *fold the paper.* Be sure he does not fold the paper unless you tell him to do so.

Word Omissions

- Sing *Old MacDonald had a* _____, *Mary had a little* _____. Say, *the boy wears a* _____ (hat). Give a visual clue by pointing to the hat in a picture. Reward the child when he supplies the missing word.

Yes or No Questions

- Use the child's vocabulary and the subjects learned: body parts, fruit, animals, colors, shapes. Ask nonsense questions: *Do feet talk? Do apples sing? Is this a circle* (point to a square)? Give the child some clues with your facial expressions.

Tell a One- to Two-Line Story

- Ask questions. Use vocabulary learned. Use flannel board for visual clues. *Mommy mailed a letter in the mailbox. The mailman took the letter to grandma. Who mailed the letter? Where did she mail the letter? Who took the letter?*

Guessing Game

- *I saw a moo in the barn. I saw a bow-bow (a meow) in the yard.* Ask the child what it is.

Riddles

- Say, *I'm thinking of a fruit which is red, sweet, and round, and it grows on trees. What is it?* Use this activity with animals, food, clothes. Say, *I see something that is round, and brown, and can bounce and rolls. What is it?* Use objects in the immediate environment.

Sorting Games

- Have each child hold a colored shape at your request. Say, *Show me a yellow square.* Remind the children to listen to the command. Place various colored circles on the floor. Say, *Jump to the red circle. Jump to the blue circle.* Play the same game with squares or triangles and with two different shapes of the same color. Gradually increase the difficulty by varying the the shapes and colors. Child must jump only on command.

- Say, *Put the green buttons in this box and the yellow buttons in that box.* Say, *Put red circles in this box and green squares in that box.* Use a combination of colors and shapes.

Auditory Discrimination

- Use loud and soft sounds introduced as big and small sounds. When music is played loud, children walk tall with hands up high over their heads. When music is played soft, children make themselves smaller. Use xylophone, piano, clapping.

- Identification of familiar sounds: record on tape or language master. Children should be able to identify, imitate, or pantomime the sounds heard. Use household sounds (running water, vacuum cleaner, flushing toilet, telephone, horn, train, plane, siren); voices (teachers, baby); animal sounds (cat, dog, cow, pig); and fast and slow sounds, or rhythms.

- Walk with slow music, run to fast music. Musical chairs: children move around chairs while music plays and sit when music stops. Alternate tempo of music between slow and fast. Children clap hands according to commands *fast* and *slow, loud* and *soft*. Remind the children to *Listen To Me*.

- Record various musical sounds on a tape recorder or the language master. Have the various instruments within the child's reach. First the child should listen to the sound. Then he may play the instrument which makes that sound. Say, *Don't touch. Listen first*. Use xylophone, bells, blocks, whistler, and crushed paper. Activity can be done with sounds which the child can repeat, such as coughing, sneezing, and clapping.

AUDITORY ASSOCIATION

Auditory association is the child's ability to relate to spoken words in a meaningful way. It is a more complicated task than auditory reception, but very important in the development of language. The child who is skilled in the auditory association area is able to understand the spoken word, to use it at different times, and to make good associations with the word (cold is associated with coat, hot is associated with iron, stove).

The process of associating words is most complicated for the trainable mentally retarded child, but it can be developed and helped by the activities suggested below.

Prior to the associating stage, the *opposite* or *finding differences* activities should be practiced. It appears to be easier on the child to find the different objects and pictures. The meaning of different can be taught with the help of visual clues such as all buttons are red but one which is green. *Which button is different? Why?* Emphasize the difference in color. Now put all green buttons in the green box and the red buttons in the red box, teaching the child to associate the matched colors.

Always emphasize short and precise verbal comments on difference and sameness. Gradually present more complicated auditory associations reinforced by visual clues (pictures, clothes, etc.).

Sorting

- Sort big items (i.e. buttons) into a big box and small items into a small box.

Finding Differences

- Point out differences between a picture of a girl and a boy, such as hair and clothing. Point out differences among children. Example: two girls face the class, and the children describe the differences between them which they observe (length of hair, type of clothing, colors of hair and clothes).

What Happens When?

- Ask the child what happens when you don't go potty, you don't wash your hands, you don't tie your shoes.

Completion of Short Phrases Without Visual Clue

- Encourage the child to complete short phrases based on daily routines. *When you get up in the morning, you*_____ (brush teeth, comb hair). Use the above activity for *I* and *me*. *When I get up,* _____. *When we get up,* _____.

Completion of Rhymes

- Have the child complete familiar rhymes, such as *One, Two, Buckle My*_____ (shoe).

Completion of Riddles

- Ask the child to complete analogous statements about familiar things, i.e. *The bird flies in air; the fish swims in*_____ (water).

Completion of One- to Two-Line Story

- Tell a short story, then show a picture for visual reinforcement. Show the picture only after you have finished and children have listened to the story. Use several picture cards to tell story and then let the child select final picture card to finish story.

Association Games

- Have pictures of different animals. Place them on a flannel board. Say, *Milk, who gives milk?* The child should point to the cow. Repeat until the child learns to associate milk with cow. Use this method with other subjects, such as clothes and parts of body (shoe—foot, hat—head). Also associate furniture with rooms (bed—bedroom, potty—bathroom).

- Have pictures of different animals displayed. Imitate animal's sounds. The child should be able to associate and name the animal with the correct sound. Use this activity with vehicles. Associate clothing with weather. Associate clothes with parts of the body. Use negative approach to elicit correct response. Say, *Do we wear shoes on our head?* (No, we wear shoes on our feet.) Associate different facial expressions with different moods. Draw (blackboard picture) happy face and talk about smiling, laughing, and how people feel when they are happy. Present the question, *When are people happy?* Draw a sad face and talk about crying, sadness, sorry, and how people feel when they are sad. Associate a mood with an event or action (birthday, falling down).

What Does Not Belong

- *What does not belong with the others?* Discuss *why*. Have squares and a circle or two triangles and a square. Use this activity with two red squares and a blue square, three green circles and a red circle.

- Use this activity with other subjects such as *fruits* (two apples and a banana), *vegetables, furniture, clothes,* and *kitchen utensils.*

Opposites

- Use the picture cards with opposite concepts. Example of opposite concepts are dirty—clean, open—shut, small—big, on—under, in—out, empty—full, wet—dry.

AUDITORY MEMORY

Auditory memory is the child's ability to remember, recall, and correctly repeat what he hears. The child must remember the sounds that make up words in order to use them again. Auditory memory is a most deficient area in the trainable mentally retarded child. Unfortunately, it is the very basis of language use and should therefore be given special consideration.

The *recall* training activities are most helpful in developing auditory memory skills. *Recall* includes the *5 W* questions below:

Who (is missing)?
What (is missing)?
When (did we go)?
Where (is my shoe)?
Why (are you crying)?

Training should begin with questions that elicit the most obvious answers, such as *What is your name? What is my name?*

Imitative games are enjoyable. Imitate animal sounds, such as *Moo*, and check the child's memory by asking him, *Who says moo?*

Proceed to more detailed questions and answers such as questioning about a very short story (2 to 3 lines) you tell the child.

Always repeat and reinforce. Variations of these activities are recommended for motivating the child and maintaining his interest.

Recall Names

- Give the child practice in remembering names of children in the classroom. Say, *Who is missing today? Whose turn is it to feed the fish? Whose turn is it to hold the flag?*

Recall Familiar Items

- Ask the child to remember things from his daily routine, such as *What do we eat with? What do we sit on?*

Recall Sounds

- Record familiar sounds, play them back, and ask the child to imitate when you name the source of the sounds. Record *Moo.* Say, *Cow.* Children should respond with *Moo.*

Recall Songs and Rhymes

- Choose songs with sequence, such as *Old Mac-Donald* and *The Wheels on the Bus.* Choose rhymes such as *One, Two, Buckle My Shoe* and *1,2,3,4,5, Once I Caught a Fish Alive.*

Recall Vehicles

- Ask the children to recall various recorded vehicle sounds.

Recall Directions

- Begin with simple directions, such as *Go get the*

ball. Proceed with more complicated directions. Ask the child to follow your directions.

Recall Geometric Shapes

- Have the child answer your questions about familiar shapes. *What is shaped like a ball? What is shaped like a box? Let's make a train—What shapes do we need?*

Recall A Short Story

- Tell a short story in sequence (daily routine). Ask questions without visual clues. You may give auditory clues by saying the initial part of the word or by asking leading questions.

Recall Digits

- Each child is assigned a telephone number. The teacher dials a number. The child stands up when his number is called. Ask, *What comes after 2? Before three?*

GRAMMATIC CLOSURE

Grammatic closure is the child's ability to use, automatically, parts of speech and grammar. The child comes to expect or predict grammatic forms, so that when part of an expression is presented, he closes the gap by supplying the missing part *Here is an apple, here are two_____* (apples).

The trainable mentally retarded child is quite deficient in this area especially in using pronouns, plurals, and prepositions.

Grammatic closure cannot be taught directly, but specially designed games and other activities should be used as indirect teaching methods.

Completion of Familiar Songs

• Old Mac_____ had a F_____. Twinkle, Twin_____ little S_____.

Differences

• Say, *These are different because_____. These are alike because_____. Say, They both have _____. _____does not belong there because _____.* Attempt to get the child to point out and verbalize the differences.

Opposites

• Say, *I open the door, now the door is opened. We get up in the morning, we go to sleep at night.* Encourage the child to repeat the whole sentence.

Plurals

• Teach the child plurals with familiar items such as body parts: tooth—teeth, foot—feet, ear—ears, eye—eyes, nose—noses.

Singular and Plural Pictures

• Use activity with subjects such as animals, fruits, clothes, and other items from the immediate environment. Do this activity individually and in unison. Be sure that the children repeat after you.

Prepositions

- Demonstrate prepositional relationships to the child. For example, *The Jack is in the box* (on, under, behind, in front of, or between). Have the child repeat and demonstrate.

Pronouns

- Demonstrate use of pronouns. Say, *This is my nose, this is your nose* (your, this, mine, our, their). Have the child repeat your words and imitate your actions.

AUDITORY CLOSURE

Auditory closure is the child's ability to predict the ending of a word, based on hearing the word in the past.

The auditory closure training activities suggested below are used to maintain and reinforce listening behavior which is most important for the development of language.

The activities are to be used with trainable mentally retarded children as fun games. They are recommended only for high-level trainables who have sufficient vocabulary and listening skills.

Visual clues (pictures) are to be given with beginning activities and dropped when children are familiar with the pictures and words.

Completing Games

- Say, *Who am I calling? Come here Bren____* (Brenda). Practice with the child's name. Give clues by looking at the child whose name you are calling. Use the same method with various items in the immediate environment. Say, *I sit on the cha____* (chair). Use this game for other subjects, such as food, clothes, animals, colors, and shapes.

- Say, *I see a roos____* (rooster). Show the picture card for a clue. Work on 2 or 3 pictures at a time. Repeat the activity until child learns the game.

- Say part of a word without presenting a visual clue. Have the child finish the word or words.

- Work on new names only after the old ones are stabilized.

Omissions

- Omit the final sounds of familiar words at first. The initial sounds used should be visible, as /p/, /b/, /m/, /w/. Then omit initial sounds; use picture cards for clues (/oat__boat). Omit medial sound; cho____lat (chocolate).

Completion of Rhymes

- One, Two, Buckle My Shoe____.

Negative Approach

- *This is not a ch____* (chair). *This is a tab____* (table). Children should repeat the above statement individually, even if the activity is done in a group.

I'm Thinking of Something

- Tell the child that you are thinking of something that is green, you write on it with ch____ (chalk). Blackboard. Use motions or picture cards to encourage responses.

VISUAL RECEPTION

Visual reception is the child's ability to comprehend actions, pictures, and other things he sees in his environment.

The trainable mentally retarded child shows deficiency in visual reception. The training activities listed below are especially designed to help the child in the development of this deficient area.

Visual reception is closely related to the trainable mentally retarded language learning process. Because of the child's limitations, it is necessary to use a multiple-sensory approach involving all the senses possible in the activity. (If the child is taught the word flower let him say it, see it, touch it, and smell it.) Pictures, films, and television programs are common techniques employed by the parent and the teacher of the trainable mentally retarded and are often found to be boring by the children. It is most probably the lack of understanding of the meaning of the picture that brings the boredom. The children do not understand what they see.

The visual reception training activities will help the parent and the teacher in teaching the child to see and understand what he sees.

Be My Shadow

- Ask the child to imitate you as you touch different body parts. Have the child imitate you as you form various shapes in the air with your finger. The song, *This is the Way I Make a Circle,* may be sung.

Can You Make A Necklace Like Mine

- Use beads and buttons to make a pattern. Increase difficulty (i.e. blue bead, red bead, three blue beads, one red bead, three blue beads).

Table Setting

- Ask the child to set a table from a model provided by a picture.

I See . . .

- Say, *I see*. Point to various items. Ask the child to say the item's name.

- Say, *I see two* _____ (shoes). Ask the child to point to shoes.

- Supply visual clues by showing pictures. Say, *I see something that is long and yellow, and it is fruit* (banana). Say, *I see one shoe, two shoes; one nose, two noses.* Emphasize numbers.

What Is Missing

- Have various items displayed. Ask the child to close his eyes. Hide one of the items. Ask the child to identify the missing object. Use shapes and different colored objects.

- Have a picture of a boy which is missing some body parts, different incomplete shapes, and pictures to be put together. The child should identify the missing parts.

Find A Common Object

- Display various picture cards, such as transportation pictures. Ask the child to point to all vehicles on wheels. Apply the above activity to other subjects, as animals (all animals with tails) and fruits (all fruits that grow on trees).

Lights Game

- Red light means stop; green light means go. The child walks and responds appropriately to signs. Begin with oral clue. Say, *Stop*, when showing the red sign. Proceed with the visual clue only. Remind the child to look at you.

Stop Sign

- The child moves from chair to chair (like musical chairs) and stops (sits) when the stop sign is raised.

Matching Actions

- Use action cards of familiar activities in the child's daily routine. Have the child pantomime the activity. Suggested activities: go to sleep, wash hands, comb hair, talk on telephone.

Matching Pictures

- Have two similar cards for each familiar item to be matched. Subjects suggested are foods, clothing household utensils, transportation, colors, and shapes. Match big spots with big spots, small with small.

More Matching Games

- Match red beads with red buttons; red squares with red circles.

- Have paired cards, some with stripes and some with spots. Ask the child to match them.

- Have green squares with red squares, etc.

Matching Concrete Pictures with Less Concrete Pictures

- Begin with identical pictures of apples. Proceed with somewhat different picture (colorless). Increase difficulty by using dotted pictures (mimeographed).

Match Dots to Numbers

- Use felt numbers in different colors and different colored dots. Instruct the children to match colors as well as numbers.

Identification Games

- Associate facial expression with moods. Have the child identify the mood.

- Present colored slides taken in the school. Ask the children to identify you, themselves, others, and classroom.

- Have different names printed on cards. The child should identify his own name.

- Ask, *Do you have this letter in your name?* Have a mineographed chart with different letters. Ask the child to circle the letters that appear in his name.

Big, Bigger, Biggest

- Have different size horses, cats, etc., on picture cards. Say, *This is big, that horse is even bigger, and this one is the biggest.*

Describe A Toy

- You describe a toy and ask child to guess what it is. The described picture cards are displayed so the child can refer to them. Ask the child to describe a toy while he looks at the picture card.

VISUAL ASSOCIATION

Visual association is the child's ability to relate visual symbols in a meaningful way.

The trainable mentally retarded child demonstrates deficiency in visual association. When given a picture of a hat among two other pictures—a bus and a man's head—he is unable to associate the hat and its proper place—the man's head.

Visual association is most important for the language development of the trainable mentally retarded child. If the child is able to make the simple association, remembering will be easier for him. One picture will remind him of the other and by doing so stimulate and reinforce his memory.

Sorting Games

- Tell the child, *Put all balls in this box and all blocks in that box. Put all blue balls in this box and all red balls in that box. Put all circles in the round box and all squares in the square box. Put all blue circles in the blue box and all red circles in the red box.*

- Have picture cards displaying summer and winter clothes. Tell the child, *Put all summer clothes here and all winter clothes there.* You may supply visual clues, such as a picture of a snow man and a swimming pool.

Pairs

- Have two identical picture cards for the children to match, such as two cups and two spoons. Have two pictures of the same items—a concrete (colorful) picture and a shadowed (black and white) picture. The children should match the two pictures. Have two pictures of the same items—a concrete (colorful) picture and a dotted picture. The children should match the two pictures.

Matching

- Have clothing articles to pass among children. When shirt is introduced, child should point to his own shirt.

Clothes To Wear

- Ask, *What do you wear on your head (feet, etc.)?* The child must select the appropriate item from a mixed pile.

More Matching

- Show the child a picture of a worker and ask him to match it with the thing that the worker does or where he works. Some examples are milk—milkman, mail—mailman, nurse—hospital, cutting hair—barber.

- Show pictures of animals and pictures of the homes where they live. Ask the child to match the animal with its home.

- Have toy furniture to be matched with the appropriate rooms in a doll's house. Use a specific color for each room as a visual clue. Then use these materials without color clue.

- Have a variety of items characteristic of different stores. Example: shoe store, mail from post office. Children should match item with corresponding picture of the store.

Simple Association

- Mix various picture cards and ask the children to associate. Use body parts and matching clothing, such as hat—head shoe—foot, glasses —eyes.

- Have a Happy Box and Sad Box with pictures indicating type of box. Give the children various expression pictures (facial). Children must match card to box. Increase difficulty presenting action cards. The child then must associate the action with the Happy or Sad box. Example: a picture of a child falling off a bike or cutting a finger would go in the sad box.

What Is Missing

- Have a few items in a box. Hide one and ask children to identify missing object. Mimeograph a picture of a boy or girl. Omit a few parts of the body. Children should identify the missing parts.

Finding Differences

- Have similar pictures with some obvious differences (two boys with different shirts). Use this activity with less obvious differences.

- Have two red balls and a green block. Have child select the different item. Increase difficulty by using different objects with same color (two red balls and one red block).

- Have two circles and a triangle. Child selects the different item. Have two noisemakers and a third item that does not make noise. Children should select odd item and discuss differences. Difference can be in construction, size, shape, color or purpose.

Opposites

- Introduce concepts on, under, in, out, up, down, dirty, clean, hot, cold, big, and small. Present appropriate opposite picture cards.

Sequential Short Story

- Present three or four pictures telling a story. Mix them up and ask child to arrange in proper sequence.

VISUAL MEMORY

Visual memory is the child's ability to remember

objects, pictures, and people he has seen before and to recall their looks from his memory (without seeing them again).

The trainable mentally retarded child is most deficient in visual memory skills which are part of the general marked deficiency in memory span that he demonstrates.

The visual memory training activities listed below are most important for the development and the reinforcement of visual memory skills. The child remembers the spoken word much better when he sees a visual clue of the picture (saying *dog* and showing the picture of a dog). Seeing an object will remind the child of its proper name and make the spoken word more meaningful to him.

Matching

- Use different color beads to string in pattern. Ask the child, *Can you make a necklace like mine?* Increase difficulty by presenting a more complicated pattern.

- Ask the child to match the right furniture set with its corresponding room (use a doll's house.)

- Use a pegboard to display a peg design. The child should match a produced design, such as triangle or square.

- Cut different shapes from construction paper and produce a pattern. The child should imitate your pattern without looking at it. Increase difficulty by increasing the number of pieces.

Recall

- Ask the child questions that will help him remember. Example: *Who is missing today* (referring to the children in the classroom)? *Who was missing yesterday? Who is my helper today* (assuming that the children take turns in setting the table, cleaning, etc.)?

- Display items, then hide them and ask the child for the missing items.

- Produce a simple colored-block pattern. Have the children verbalize the order of the pattern without looking at it. Present picture cards in sequential order. Hide one of the pictures. The children must supply the missing picture (children verbalize). Increase difficulty by questioning in greater details.

- *Let's make a train (a house, a snowman).* Have the children supply the right shapes (squares and circles for the train, etc.).

- Mimeograph a picture missing some obvious details. Use pictures of body parts.

Following Orders

- Say, *Touch the color I name.* The children must run in the room, and find and touch the color called.

- *Stop!* The children must listen and stop the activity (running, walking), when the stop sign is shown.

- Draw on the floor with chalk a square, a circle,

and a triangle. Give a short command, *Jump to the circle.* The children follow your command. Draw different color shapes using the above activity on a more difficult level.

VISUAL CLOSURE

Visual closure is the child's ability to identify a common object from an incomplete visual presentation.

The trainable mentally retarded child shows general deficiency in visual skills especially when concentration is required. His attention span is very short, and it is most difficult for him to look for parts of objects and identify them (a dog's tail should remind him of a dog).

The visual closure activities listed below are used for the development of better looking behavior and longer concentration ability which are essential for the development of language.

Puzzles

- Begin with two-piece or three-piece puzzles, increase difficulty by increasing pieces.

- Cut a picture card in half, mix with other pieces. Children should match and put pieces together to form the original cards.

- Match colored puzzle pieces with corresponding color on margin.

Incomplete Picture

- Present an incomplete picture and ask children to verbalize missing parts.

Dotted Objects

- Mimeograph dotted fruit and shapes. Children should complete the forms by connecting the dots.

Hidden Objects

- Hide a shoe behind a chair. Leave it partially visable. Children should find the hidden object. Use this technique in a picture. Draw part of an item as if hiding behind another item. Children should point to the hidden object.

Geometric Shapes

- Use the flannel board. Have half circles and quarter circles. Assemble three-quarters of circle, have child complete. Use blackboard. Draw part of shape and have child complete.

Chapter IV

BASIC VOCABULARY RELATED TO DAILY LIVING ACTIVITIES

FAMILY

Mommy

Daddy

Brother

Sister

grandmother

grandfather

other relatives

specific names of family
members

child's own name

HEALTH

potty—toilet—bathroom

wash hands

wash face

bath

towel

soap

dry hands

comb hair

brush teeth

dirty

nice-and-clean

sink

bathtub

BODY IDENTIFICATION

head

mouth

cheeks

feet

eyes

ears

hands

toes

nose

chin

fingers

thumb

tummy

elbow

knee

ankle

GREETINGS AND MANNERS

hi

bye

please

thank you

you're welcome

may I

FOOD

eat

spoon

drink

table

chair

glass

fork

knife

plate

bowl

names of favorite foods,
    fruits, vegetables, drinks, etc.

CLOTHES

shoe

boot

sock

pants (slacks)

shirt

blouse

skirt

dress

coat

jacket

snow suit

hat, cap

mittens

scarf

pocketbook

WORDS FOR PROTECTION

no

hot

don't touch

stop

come here

sit down

get up

go

SCHOOL

school

children

teacher

quiet

bus

bye-bye

lunch

HOLIDAYS

Christmas	tree
Santa Claus	party
sock	Valentine
reindeer	pumpkin
presents	Thanksgiving
flag	pilgrim

BIRTHDAY

age (how old)	party
candles	present
cake	Happy Birthday To You

ANIMALS

farm animals (i.e. cow, pig, duck, horse, goat, sheep, chicken)
pets—home animals (i.e. dog, cat, fish, bird)
zoo animals (i.e. lion, monkey, tiger)

COLORS

names of colors (red, blue, green, yellow, etc.)
identification (*What color is this? Show me the blue ball.*)

COMMUNITY HELPERS

barber	school
policeman	nurse
fireman	doctor
mailman	hospital
post office	dentist
teacher	

DAILY ROUTINES

get up	go to school
lunch	good morning
dress (wear)	wash
good night	go to sleep
dinner	potty—toilet—bathroom

SHAPES

circle	triangle
square	rectangle
round	

HOME

address (street, number, town)	bathroom
phone number	garage
kitchen	stove
bedroom	sink
bed	refrigerator
chair	telephone
couch	television
radio	table

SEASONS

winter	hat
spring	boots
summer	socks
fall (autumn)	snowsuit
outside	sneakers
rain	mittens
snow	hat
cold	swim
coat	flowers
inside	bathing suit

TOYS AND GAMES

puzzle	doll
book	truck
blocks	names of favorite toys and games
sing	
car	names of playmates

Chapter V

BASIC LANGUAGE CONCEPTS

THIS BASIC LANGUAGE concept list was found to be of common use in the everyday language of the trainable mentally retarded child at home and in school. It is not meant to suggest that these concepts should be taught directly. The concepts should be learned and used through everyday usage. The parent and the teacher of the trainable mentally retarded child should keep these usable concepts in mind and emphasize and reinforce them through home and school activities. The basic list is as follows:

big—small	dirty—clean
up—down	stop—go
on—under	wet—dry
in—out	run—walk
open—shut	eat—drink
hot—cold	empty—full
loud—quiet	soft—hard

Big . . . Small

- Show the child differences in pictures: big dog—small dog. Use one item in different sizes.

- Show the child differences in his immediate environment: big chair—small chair.

- Have the child match big buttons with a big box and small buttons with a small box.

- Show the child the difference between big and small by cutting out big circles and small circles. Have the child compare them by putting the small one on top of the big one. Use squares and triangles.

- With a piece of chalk, draw a big circle and a small circle on the floor. Ask the child to jump to the big circle, the small circle.

Up . . . Down

- Play games with the child in which he is directed to fall down and get up. One such game is *Ring Around Rosie*.

- Throw things in the air that are familiar to the child. Say, *I am throwing ___ up. ___ is coming down.* Encourage the child to repeat your words.

- Play *Simon Says*. When the child can repeat your actions, test his comprehension of up and down by instructing him orally without visual clue.

- Hold your hand up. Ask the child, *Where is my hand?*

On . . . Under

- Place a toy on the table or chair. Ask the child, *Where is the toy?* When the child verbalizes the correct concept, allow him to take the toy.

- Instruct the child to place his hands on the table, under the table.

- Instruct the child to place the block on the box, under the box.

- Instruct the child to place one set of things on and another set of things under (i.e. *place the red circle on the box and place the blue circles under the box.*

In . . . Out

- Instruct the child to put the blocks in the box or take the blocks out of the box.

- Play *garage.* Have the child put his car in the garage and take his car out of the garage.

- Play *dolls.* Have the child put her doll in the crib or carriage and take her doll out of the crib or carriage.

- Emphasize the concepts in and out in your lessons (i.e. The cow is in the barn. The chicken is in the chicken house. Mommy is in the house. Daddy is out working.) .

Open . . . Shut

- Sing the song, *Open shut them, open shut them, put them in your lap.* Accompany your singing with the appropriate motions (open and shut your hands) .

- What is missing? The child must identify the missing object, but also respond to *shut your eyes* and *open your eyes* when he is told to.

- Emphasize: *open* the door, *shut* the door.

Hot . . . Cold

- Learning from touching experience: touch hot water and say *hot,* hot food, etc.
- The child feels a cold bottle on his cheek and repeats after you, *cold.*
- Emphasize: *It's cold, put your coat on!*
- Remind the child and emphasize *hot* when you iron or cook (stove is on, etc.) .

Loud . . . Quiet

- The whispering game: say, *Talk quietly.* Pass a word quietly from child to child.
- The echoing game: say a word loudly and immediately echo your own word quietly.
- Record loud and quiet music. When music is played, ask the children to tell you when it is loud and when it is quiet.
- Emphasize *Be quiet* during nap time. Emphasize louder when children sing.

Dirty . . . Clean

- Emphasize dirty hands after coming from the play outdoors. Emphasize clean hands after washing.
- Emphasize, clean shirt when child comes to school in the morning. Point to dirty shirt when it is dirty.
- Point to the dirty table after lunch. Ask the children to clean the table, emphasizing clean after they have done their job.

Stop . . . Go

- Instruct the children to listen to your command. Upon *Go,* children should start walking. Walk with them, giving an example. Upon *stop,* children must stop and remain standing in their places.
- If children recognize the stop sign, you may use it for signaling *Stop.*
- Emphasize stop to stop undersirable behavior.

Wet . . . Dry

- Emphasize wet when the child wets his pants.
- Emphasize dry when the child dries his hands.
- Wash baby clothes in the classroom. Hang the clothes on a rope, touching it often and saying, *Wet.*
- Children imitate the teacher.
- When clothes dry, children take them off the rope.

Run . . . Walk

- Instruct the children about a run—walk game. When you say, *Run,* everybody runs, including the teacher who supplies the visual clue to the command.
- At a later stage, instruct the children orally without doing so yourself.
- Play the game of running to the table, balancing a book on your head, and walking slowly back trying to keep the book balanced.

Eat . . . Drink

- Emphasize eating with teeth, drinking with tongue.

- Practice the mouth motions when eating (chewing) and drinking (formation of lips). Let the children experiment with the two concepts.

- Tell them, *Try and drink your meat* or *Try and eat your milk;* make it a fun game.

Empty . . . Full

- Associate empty with all gone and slowly increase the usage of empty (rather than all gone). Show the child the empty bottle or box.

- Ask, *What's in the box?* The child answers, *Nothing, the box is empty.*

- Before lunch emphasize empty tummy. After lunch emphasize full tummy.

- Play with the child in a sand box, filling and emptying containers. Use negative approach: Point to the full container and ask, *Is this empty?* The child should answer, *No it's full.*

Soft . . . Hard

- Feeling various items such as wool and stones, discuss the different items in terms of hardness and softness.

- Discuss the difference between a plastic ball, wooden ball, and cloth ball in terms of hardness and softness.

- Knock on the table, saying, *Hard.*
- Pat the toy dog's hair, saying, *Soft.*
- Alternate snacks between hard ice cream and soft ice cream.

BIBLIOGRAPHY

Buddenhagen, Ronald G.: *Establishing Vocal Verbalization in Mute Mongoloid Children*. Illinois, Research Press, 1971.

Dunn, Lloyd M., Horton, Kathryn, and Smith, James O.: *Peabody Language Development Kits. Manual for level # P*. Minnesota, American Guidance Service, 1968.

Greene, Margaret C. L.: *Learning to Talk. A Parent's Guide to the First Five Years*. New York, Harper & Brothers, 1960.

Illingworth, R. S.: How to help a child achieve his best. *J. Pediatrics, 73*:60–8. 1968.

Irwin, Ruth B.: *A Speech Pathologist Talks to Parents and Teachers*. Pittsburg, Stanwix House, 1962.

Karlin, I. W., and Strazzulla, M.: Speech and language problems of mentally deficient children. *J. Speech Hearing Dis., 17,* 1952.

Karnes, Merle B.: *Helping Young Children Develop Language Skills. A Book of Activities*. Washington, D.C., 1968.

McCarthy, James J., Kirk, Samuel A., and Kirk, Winifred D.: *Illinois Test of Psycholinguistic Ability*. Board of Trustees, University of Illinois, 1968.

Molloy, Julia S.: *Trainable Children Curriculum and Procedures*. New York, John Day, 1963.

Myklebust, Helmer R.: *Auditory Disorders in Children. A Manual for Differential Diagnosis*. New York, Grune and Stratton, 1969.

Santin, Sylvia E.: *Speech and Language Activities for the Trainable Retarded Child*. Toronto, Metropolitan Toronto Association for the Mentally Retarded, 1969.

Schiffer, Mortimer: *The Therapeutic Play Group*. New York, Grune & Stratton, 1969.

Skinner, B. F.: *Verbal Behavior.* New York, Appleton, 1957.

Staats, Arthur W.: *Learning, Language and Cognition. Theory, Research, and Method for the Study of Human Behavior and Its Development.* New York, Holt, Rinehart and Winston, 1968.

Travis: *Handbook of Speech Pathology.* New York, Appleton-Century-Crofts, 1957.

Van Riper, Charles: *Speech Correction, Principles and Methods.* Englewood Cliffs, N.J., Prentice-Hall, 1961.

Van Riper, Charles: *Teaching Your Child to Talk.* New York, Harper & Brothers, 1950.

Van Riper, Charles: *Your Child's Speech Problems.* New York, Harper & Brothers, 1961.

Wood, Nancy E.: *Delayed Speech and Language Development.* Englewood Cliffs, N.J., Prentice-Hall, 1964.

GLOSSARY

Auditory association—the child's ability to relate spoken words in a meaningful way.

Auditory closure—child's ability to predict the ending of a word, based on hearing the word in part.

Auditory discrimination—the ability to note small differences in sounds.

Auditory memory—the child's ability to remember, recall, and correctly repeat what he hears.

Auditory reception—the child's ability to understand what is said to him.

Auditory trainer—a device designed to produce amplification of sounds for the hard-of-hearing.

Cerebral palsy—an inability to control one's movement and speech, due to damage to the brain before or during birth.

C.A. (chronological age)—the child's calendar age. A chronological age (C.A.) of 6-9, for example, means that a child is 6 years, 9 months old.

Grammatic closure—the child's ability to use, automatically, parts of speech and grammar.

Hypotonic swallower—a child who has not learned how to swallow properly, thereby producing a constant drooling.

Jaw stability—the ability to control the muscles in the jaw area and to hold it in its proper place.

Language master—a machine which operates on the basis of a tape recorder using special cards which can provide instant replay of specific sounds.

Lip closure—ability to close lips properly and maintain that position for a suitable length of time.

Medial—of or in the middle.

Memory span—the length of time that the child can remember what has been learned.

M.A. (mental age)—level of intellectual development expressed as equivalent to the average of a particular chronological age group, usually as reflected in test scores.

Mongolism (Down's syndrome)—the largest single syndrome accompanied by severe retardation. Mongoloid children are characterized by speech disorders and a coarse, low-pitched voice.

Motivation—an incentive or interest in learning.

Motor—having to do with movements of the muscles.

Motor behavior—the ability of the body and body organs to move properly.

Multiple-sensory approach—motivating the child by employing all senses possible.

Operant conditioning—the use of reward and punishment to encourage desirable behavior and discourage undesired behavior.

Perception—the process of organizing and interpreting sensory data (sights, sounds, body position, etc.) by combining them with the results of past experience.

Psycholinguistic—an approach sometimes used in language training.

Receptive language—the understanding of the spoken words.

Reflex closure—an uncontrolled reaction bringing the mouth to a close.

Reinforcement—act of strengthening what has been learned.

Self-image—how the child sees himself or feels about himself.

Sensory—sight, sound, smell; involving all sense organs (mouth, nose, hands, etc.) .

Speech—the oral process of communication; the actual speaking of words.

Tactile—the feeling by touch.

Tongue control—the ability to hold the tongue in the mouth and to move it in the directions necessary to help in the production of speech.

Trainable mentally retarded—a term used to refer to mentally retarded persons whose disabilities are such that they are incapable of meaningful achievement in academic subjects, but who are capable of profiting from programs of training in self-care, social, and simple job skills.

Visual association—the child's ability to relate visual symbols in a meaningful way.

Visual closure—the child's ability to identify a common object from an incomplete visual presentation.

Visual memory—the child's ability to remember objects, pictures, and people he has seen before and to recall their looks from his memory.

Visual reception—the child's ability to comprehend actions, pictures, and other things he sees in his environment.

Visual sounds—a sound which causes immediate association with an object, either through picture identification or memory (for example, *moo*).

INDEX

A

Activities, training, *see* Training
activities
Auditory association, 27–31
training activities for, 29–31
association games, 29, 30
differences, finding, 28
opposites, use of, 31
phrases, short, completion of, 29
sorting, 28
rhymes, completion of, 29
riddles, completion of, 29
story, completion of, 29
what does not belong, 30
what happens when, 29
Auditory closure, 35–37
training activities for, 35–37
completing games, 35
I'm thinking of something, 36, 37
negative approach, 36
omissions, word, 36
rhymes, completion of, 36
Auditory clues, 33, 39
Auditory memory, 31–33
training activities for, 32–33
digits, recall of, 33
directions, simple, recall of, 32, 33
geometric shapes, recall of, 33
items, familiar, recall of, 32
names, recall of, 32
songs and rhymes, recall of, 32
sounds, recall of, 32
story, short, recall of, 33
vehicles, recall of, 32
Auditory reception, 20, 23, 24, 27
training activities for, 24–27
auditory discrimination, 26, 27
body parts, identification of, 24
directions, more complicated,
following of, 24

directions, simple, following
of, 24
guessing game, 25
paper folding, 25
questions, yes or no, 25
riddles, 26
sorting games, 26
word omission, 25

B

Breathing, proper, 3
see also Inhaling exercises,
Exhaling exercises

C

Chewing, 4, 6, 18, 58
training activities for, 7

D

Drooling, control of, 4, 17
training activities for, 6

E

Exercises, training, *see* Training
activities
Exhaling exercises, 4, 5
Expressive language, *see* Language,
expressive

G

Games, 8, 11, 12, 25, 54, 56
see also Training activities
Goals, language development, *see*
Language development goals
Grammatic closure, 33–35
training activities for, 34–35
differences, finding, 34
opposites, use of, 34